Child, I Will Always Carry You

"Meg Smith's poems touch the heart and move the spirit, not by posturing and presenting grand, abstract themes, but by celebrating the small, intimate, heart-tugging and often humorous moments in a woman's life, particularly a mother's life: practical wisdom learned from grandmothers and imparted to daughters, secrets kept, rueful apologies made. These seemingly small moments are enlarged by Smith's cleareyed vision and generous imagination—they become sacramental moments, imparting their sweet, simple, much-needed grace. 'How lovely is your dwelling place,' one poem repeats, depicting with a few vivid details the landscapes of the poet's childhood home as well as her present home in Vermont. I would add one more 'location' to this litany: how lovely are these poems, dwelling places of spirit, which as readers we get to enter and enjoy."

—JULIA ALVAREZ,
author of *In the Time of the Butterflies*

"Here is a remarkable collection of poems pierced through with light on the wonders, griefs, and ironic moments that lie, often unnoticed and uncelebrated, within the vocation of motherhood. From a careful attentiveness to the exquisite delights that rest in nurturing young bodies and souls to the inevitable failures, Meg gives place to her own childhood, the present beauty and difficulties of mothering, and the longings for the future of her family, all held in the grace of God. Her evocative images and crisp wording penetrate the heart, remind the soul, and refresh the intentions of every mother, new and experienced."

—GAYLE HEASLIP,
Anglican Priest

"Margaret Smith's ode to motherhood is honest, tender, and alive, with language that sings. Drawing out the sacred in the ordinary, these poems read almost as short liturgies—some of praise, some of lament. Humor hides here, as does profundity. One cannot read this fine compilation without fresh gratitude for those who have mothered us and wonder at the divine design which includes all of us in the story of giving and caring for new life."

—ABIGAIL CARROLL,
author of *Cup My Days Like Water*

"We come to these poems for their mother-wonder—bedazzlement and bewilderment intermixed. Reading these poems, we are comforted to share with Meg Smith the heart feeling that all our words of beloved children feel like first words, riddled with breaking, but rich with becoming. Reading these poems, we are assured of a Lord who hears, who understands our words even before we do, who makes them into poetry."

—TIFFANY EBERLE KRINER,
Professor of English, Wheaton College

"Margaret Smith's poems offer us love without descending into mere sentimentality, pain without self-pity, and an invitation to laugh not only at the humor of parenting's obviously comic moments, but even at—perhaps especially at—the most maddening of them, making that daily chaos so much less mundane. That thread of humor adds to the poignancy of the more intimate moments as when the poet sits in the doctor's office listening to a diagnosis of a husband's cancer and notes simply that 'our lives are china tea cups / in the hands of a toddler.' You don't need to be a mother or even a parent to appreciate this beautiful collection."

—MATTHEW DICKERSON,
author of *Aslan's Breath: Seeing the Holy Spirit in Narnia*

Child, I Will Always Carry You

MEG MCFADDEN SMITH

RESOURCE *Publications* · Eugene, Oregon

CHILD, I WILL ALWAYS CARRY YOU

Resource Publications
An Imprint of Wipf and Stock Publishers
199 W. 8th Ave., Suite 3
Eugene, OR 97401

www.wipfandstock.com

PAPERBACK ISBN: 979-8-3852-4350-1
HARDCOVER ISBN: 979-8-3852-4351-8
EBOOK ISBN: 979-8-3852-4352-5

04/28/25

This book is dedicated to:

Chloe, Asher, Ewan, and Willa.
You were made in love, by love, and for love.

And to mothers, young and old, doing what love
requires. The Lord sees you.

CONTENTS

MAKE ME MONARCH

Make me monarch,
birth me from chrysalis
wet-winged, trembling in flight.

Lift me on wind,
scribble me with sun,
color me bold as fire.

Flutter me from cage,
kite me over roof,
soar me skyward.

O Lord of Winged Things,
crafter of cocoon,
sculptor of proboscis,

designer of antennae,
pilot of angels,
untether me from ground

and I will belong
to tops of trees,
Cumulus and breeze.

WHERE MIST HOVERS HOLY

How lovely is your dwelling place
at Hill House
under white oak after rain
on lawn of my childhood home
as shafts of light shine through willow
tickled by wind.

How lovely is your dwelling place
on Lake Michigan
where Midwest sun climbs high,
and waves tumble
like frollicking kids,
as day blends gently into night
and we coalesce around the campfire
singing the old songs.

How lovely is your dwelling place
on a northern Vermont plain
where hollyhocks lean,
lilies line a white fence,
Rhode Island reds roost
and children basket brown eggs.

How lovely is your dwelling place
in the North Country church of my youth
between sips of communion wine,
wafer cracking in my mouth,
chords sounding on organ,
cemetery filled with old stones.

How lovely is your dwelling place
on pine bench by Beaver Lake
folded among firs

where mist hovers holy above water
and songs echo early and late
as worship lands like dew
on every bough
and laughter shakes down
like needles in the wind.

How lovely is your dwelling place, O LORD Almighty!
—Psalm 84:1, NIV

MAKE ME SMALL

shrink my hand down
to slipping size
let it slide between
my father's fingers,
a quiet smile
curling on his cheeks
and in my heart
the start
of a song.

Make me small
just the right size
for climbing into laps
and settling smoothly
between boundaries
of my mother's body,
wombed outside womb
heated by her heat,
drummed by her breath,
her arms my barricade,
her legs my drawbridge,

and I will sit silently
sucking my thumb,
a single thought held in my head
or perhaps no thought at all,
eyes wide to world,
every detail a fresh category
of knowing, every face
opportunity for love.

SHELTER

—for Tyler

Tonight, beams of this
old farmhouse moan,
branches break and fall,
willow whips in wind,
raindrops hammer roof,
gather in gutters,
flood frozen ground.

In our bedroom
your arms wrap me,
your fingers thread
through mine, your breath
hums through the night,
while your body
warms my body
like a woodstove.

What would it be like
to sleep outdoors
in this winter storm,
to loose cocoon
of down and Eider,
to have no tent to shield
from downpour, or walls
to break the wind?

It would be like
 life
without you.

EXPECTANT

Cover mattress with yellow sheet,
fold socks that will touch tiny feet.
Prepare for life to enter the room,
feel your body swell with a full womb.

Nothing to do but watch and wait,
kin to those faithful saints
keeping watch through time, eyes wide
studying horizon for some great divide,

or subtle sign, shifting of wind,
repenting of ways they have sinned,
pressing their ears to the silent ground,
listening for rumbling sounds,

willing a great contracting of earth,
soil to split with full force of birth,
all creation to rouse from sleep,
hallelujahs to tear from deep to deep.

NEWBORN

One mild March morning
a nurse tells the professor
to cradle his infant,
and he freezes,
as if searching
for some formula
that would explain
how to hold an idea
birthed into body.

He lowers his hulk
into a rocker, bends
a hairy arm to receive
her flopping frame,
her skin sticking
to his chest hair
like a stamp to an envelope.

He fingers her toes
and rocks her gently
as tears and snot
stream down his face.

All through the night
his eyes held his wife
as she labored,
now he peers into pupils
hungry for contact,
caresses a head misshapen by birth,
her body a blueprint
of who she will become.

When it comes time
to change the first diaper
the doula teaches him how
to tell back from front, how
to fold lip under stump
of umbilical cord.

While the midwife measures
the baby on a blanket on the floor,
he lies prostrate
by his daughter,
murmuring his first words.

POSTPARTUM

Bursting from my body
you were born one morning
in a storm of energy
after your siblings
left for school.

You were pushed from me with labor pains,
my body torn because separation
does not come easy. I felt
the sweet relief of your absence.

Hours after birth you slept,
your body curled inside
invisible walls of womb,
oblivious to the space around it.

When you woke, the toes
that had poked my bladder
kicked swaddling blankets,
fingers that had floated in amniotic fluid
folded around fingers that fathered them.
The midwife checked your vitals.
The pulse that once drummed
its rhythm through Doppler
now beat outside my body.

I gathered you to my breast.
My hands held heft that my body basketed,
soul like a bowl sculpted
inside the kiln of my womb.

Hours since you rested in me
phantom kicks and jabs
disturb my uterus still.
I rest my hand on my belly,
only to remember it's empty.

Child, I will always carry you.

CROSSING THE THRESHOLD

Praise be
for hands
and how they beckon another closer
wave in welcome
intertwine two into one

      for handshake
         high five
            pound-it
               knuckles

      for lips
and ways they stamp skin
with kindness
like a notary's seal
holy anointing of friend
or grandmother or lover

      for skin to skin
      mouth to breast
melding of infant and mother
back into each other.

Praise be to the One
who coded touch
into human design,
maker of all manner of ways
for crossing the threshold
between us.

TO-DO LIST, SPRING

Open eyes. Leap from sheets.
Dash outside in bare feet.
Stare at birch's lipped buds,
stroke wooly bear's fur,
giggle at wind's tickle.

Pick bouquets of dandelions,
twirl them into strawberry hair,
stir muffins made of mud
set them to simmer in sun.
Sink seeds, those tiny wishes,
in sandy soil.

Consider whether friend or foe,
each animal one can know.
Find a mouse and let him go.
Watch him scurry, a gray blur,
ask, "Where will he sleep tonight?"

Jump on anything found.
Climb whatever legs can reach.
Howl when called inside.
Hold eyes wide while light lasts.
Surrender to sleep.

COMMUNION

I hold the bread in the hollow of my hand.
Her tiny fingers grasp
to hold the body of Christ,
she who has yet to eat bread.

I hold the chalice between my palms,
she shifts her gaze toward the cup,
makes a guttural sound,
she, who has drunk only from my breast.

Child, may you hunger for the Body,
thirst for the Blood.

Nothing else will satisfy you like these.

DAILY OFFICE

Breakfast cut bite-size
squirming body dressed,
stroller pushed in morning light —
this, my invocation.

Diapers strung on the line,
sweet potato scrubbed from plates,
soiled sheets changed —
these, my oblations.

Menu made, items listed to buy,
stories read, balls rolled,
squash soup stirred —
this, the liturgy of my days.

Toes scrubbed and washed,
lullabies sung and hopes hung
like clouds on the mobile —
this, my benediction.

I wipe my prayers over the soiled counter
and chop them with a knife,
pin them like onesies to a clothesline altar
and whisper to the passing wind —

O You who held my infancy in your hands,
receive these my offerings.

COMMON MIRACLE

Wide-eyed, he watches the feeder,
wondering,
when will the birds come?

Then, one day,
two house sparrows land,
their pinpoint beaks nibbling
one ball at a time,
sprinkling
seeds on snow.

And we, the one-year-old
who can barely see over the sill,
and the mother who has seen so much
she has lost her sight,
look on in wonder.

TOMATO HARVEST

—for Liam

Many tomatoes ripened on the vine;
the sugar-smell wafted from the row.
One green tomato fell before its time.

All through the fruit's growth there came no sign,
and now there's no replacing the one lost, though
other tomatoes hang ripe on the vine.

In a warm room the plant began the climb
from seed to shoot to vine, no way to know
it would lose one fruit before its time.

In Spring, thin shoots emerged in line,
and the green tomato began to grow
like other fruit hanging on the vine.

In late August when tomatoes are prime,
the vine without warning let the green one go
and it tumbled to the ground before its time.

Unclipping the clothes from the clothesline
I think of the baby they will not hold.
So many tomatoes ripening on the vine,
one green tomato fell before its time.

BURIAL DURING A PANDEMIC

We gather in the yard
by the daffodils,
our breath clouding
crisp air. My son
thrusts his red shovel
into sandy soil,
his small body bent in labor.

Many bodies have been buried
without a funeral, and yet
I carry the carcass of a chick
on a rough-cut board
from the scrap wood bin.

This Rhode Island Red
lies like a deflated balloon,
like so many bodies
strapped to stretchers
carried out of ICUs
and into morgues.

I tip the board,
and the cold, yellow corpse
slips into soil. The children
look at me from older eyes,
as if to ask how I could allow
such a tragedy.

In cities across our nation
there are not enough graves
to contain the remains.
The living cannot hold hands
with the dying.

We mourn for a single chick
because we cannot begin
to count all that has been lost.

APOLOGY

Dear Goldie,
I did not clean your tank
or add fresh water
or change your filter.

Goldie, please forgive me.
When you came to live with us
the three-year-old wore a red cast,
I was about to discover
I was pregnant with number four,
and you never whined
if you got too little dinner
or the wrong snack
or if the flakes failed to satisfy
your delicate Betta palette.

I'm sorry for letting kids
tap the glass, strobe your light,
for the neighbor boy dumping
a canister of BettaMin medley
in your tank. You swam
in silent (seeming) contentment
even as your world grayed,
as mold greened the walls
of your habitat. Thanksgiving week,
when my boy got pneumonia
and we mourned a dead grandmother,
I was planning to scrub your tank,
really I was, but then Sunday
before church, someone from the
mothers' prayer group found you
face down in neon orange rocks,

and I knew
I would have
to tell the children
that you had died too.

Goldie, thank you for your sacrifice.
To the end you were an uncomplaining,
blissfully quiet presence in our home.

Oh, and Goldie?
If my little boy ever
meets you in heaven
(he's hoping to find you there)
could we keep all this just between us?

THE LORD IS MY MOTHER

who picks a bouquet of lilacs
and places it on my dresser,
who strips my bed
of soiled sheets
and covers mattress
in fresh linens,
while the aroma of bread
spreads through the house.

The Lord is my mother
who draws me a warm bath,
pours water over my head
that dribbles down my cheeks
like a thousand kisses,
and when my soak is done
wraps me in a towel
heated by dryer,
and brushes tangles from my hair.

The Lord is my mother
who sleeps half-awake
listening
and when I call
strokes my forehead
wipes away visions
that lurk in darkness,
whose slow sounds soothe me
into a cadence of breath.

The Lord is my mother
who wakes before me,
meets me with open arms
in the light of morning,
pulls off the hanger
my favorite cotton sundress,
the one with yellow lilies.

NATIVITY

Where is baby Jesus?
Did someone stuff him in the couch,
stick him in blue spruce needles,
cover him with a coffee filter snowflake,
hide him in a used gift bag,
toss him out with salt dough stars?

Gabriel shouts glad tidings
to shepherds who grip fuzzy crooks.
They watch a solitary sheep
limp along on a bent pipe cleaner leg.

Wise men perch on windowsill,
removed from the scene,
and Mary leans toward Joseph,
as if whispering to him about
their missing infant.

LINES WRITTEN WHILE CLEANING

Divine Maker of All Things,
thank you for clutter,
for car-shaped slippers,
compact discs without cases,
frisbee stuck on roof,
race cars parked under pillows,
submarine capsized
on bathroom tile,
puppet hanging from noose
of the ball hoop,
stuffed frog bungeed to handlebars,
Lego men hiding out in couch bunkers,
paper airplane stranded on staircase landing strip.

Thank you for entropy,
for boots caked in mud,
crumbs squashed under table,
baking soda eruptions from volcano,
Cheerios tipped over,
red paint wiped on sink,
pepper flakes floating in bottle of green water,
cheeks kissed with ketchup,
nails polished with dirt,
grass-stained, ketchup-stained,
oil-soaked shirts.

Thank you for fingers
that shredded
newspaper into a heap,
for sticky hands
that anointed doorknob,
light switch, and faucet.

O Divine Artist,
thank you for these
ministers of mess,
my priests and priestess of play.

SONNET NUMBER FOUR

—for Tyler

For all I have not seen inside your eyes
when you needed me to stop and listen,
for my indifference to your desire
and times I lost our two-as-one vision,

forgive me. O how I fail to love you
and turn again to my own selfish ways!
With the best of intentions I said "I do,"
now you hold the record of all my days.

I do not yet know how to have, to hold,
have not learned how to give rather than take.
How do we tend our love as it grows old?
What marriage mold together shall we make?

For this breath of time before we perish,
o my lover, it's you I choose to cherish.

LEARNING TO TALK

—for Willa

She rides on my back
and over whining wind
I hear her whisper,
"Doggy"
while watching a chocolate lab
tug against its lead,
continues to word, "Doggy"
as we wind our way
down a block without any.

Their absence matters little to her,
the sighting of a single one
sustains, as does the shape
dah and *gee* form in her throat
as she plays with them,
balls tossed between tongue
and teeth, sounds smiling
back at her as she births them
into wintry air, each one
a foray into the unknown.

THE CURSE

My five-year-old first
dropped the bomb
after school
in protest
when his dad said
the grapes were gone.

The word spread
through our home
like a virus.
Before long
even the three-year-old
had been trained
in nuances of pronunciation.
No, it's not duck.
There's an f-sound.

How did my kindergartner
learn the f-word?
The answer was simple,
from another kindergartner.

I imagine the mother
of the family
where five-year-olds
learn to speak this way.

I shake my fist at her,
my imaginary villain,
enemy of children's innocence,
resistor of goodness and beauty.

Then, one snowy day,
I meet her. Her smile
spreads from cheek to cheek.
She seems more
angel than adversary.

WTF?

HOW DO YOU MEASURE A LIFE?

In pounds and ounces,
in birthdays and beats,
in sounds and syllables,
in stumbles and steps?

There's a small space
in her mouth tonight
where her baby tooth
used to be.

We waited a year
for an incisor to grow,
and she has waited
for the first one to go.

How do you capture the time?
We measured each inch
with a single line
penciled on the wall.
Somehow she slipped through
the marks we drew.

Just now she came down,
holding her trophy,
cradling six years in her palm.

PLAYING CATCH

You throw and I catch,
two simple motions that stitch
your hand to mine.

You look at me
to see
if I am watching.
I look at you,
fifteen-year-old you,
second son of my brother,
and see a toddler
wiggling his body
to a singing Christmas tree,
a young boy throwing sticks
into a Rocky Mountain stream,
one whose complaints
lengthened a short hike.

Now you have grown tall
and I have no words to say,
but I can aim this frisbee
toward you, look in your eyes,
and I know you will catch it.

OUR CONFLICT

We go to the grocery store;
I carry you in my belly.
I carry you in a frontpack.
I carry you on my hip.
Then, I hold your hand.
One day, you refuse
to hold my hand.

You seem to need
to teach me
you are separate
from me;
I seem to need
to remind you
you are part of me.

LEARNING TO RIDE

—for Chloe

There you go,
your feet pushing pedals,
your hands gripping handlebars.

Your body moves magically
without me; somehow you know
the way to make yourself go,
to balance by leaning left,
to steady by tipping right.

I remember learning to ride a bike.
I remember the thrill,
the terror, of being on my own,
suddenly released to steer my own destiny.

There you go, darling daughter,
pedaling away from me.

LEARNING TO SKATE

As we circle the rink
my children lean
on me for balance,
their bodies borrowing my body
the way they did as infants
when suckling at my breast.

My son crashes on ice
and I lift him to standing,
just as my mother lifted me,
her body rooted as I held on to her.

She seemed so secure.
I feel shaky tonight as they tug,
their weight disrupting my equilibrium,
threatening to push me off balance.

I remember after slipping along the rink
the surprise as my mother left
to skate a lap on her own.
I watched her glide away
as if seeing her for the first time,

separate from me.

THE SHORE

—for Mom

Mom was a girl at the Jersey Shore,
before Grandma installed the indoor shower.
Mom showered outside, stared up through
Atlantic air to the blueberry brook sky.

I was a girl there too, my tender soles
tiptoeing home for an after-beach rinse,
the fire of July pavement sprayed away
by nettle pressure of the hose.

Mom was a girl, her mother calling
from the kitchen, waving a wooden spoon,
reminding us sand belonged outside.
Mom rubbed our sandy feet with towels

until they smarted. My mother,
a girl, taking orders from her mother.
I was a girl too, Mom reminding me
to hang up my suit, not drip inside,

not track in sand. I ran to the clothesline,
water from my soggy suit
dripping over the flagstones.

THE ORANGE FRINGE JACKET

—for Dad and Mom

of soft, suede cloth
still hangs in their closet.
The tassels dangle down
and when she first saw him
he was wearing it
through Amsterdam town.
She noticed the coat
matched the color of his hair.

A few years later
they made their vows
to have and hold,
to carry each other
even when carrying
each other grew old;
now decades later
she still wears
that roadrunner ring.

They bought an old house
on a North Country hill
where summer breeze
blows through corn,
primrose and lilies grow,
and they planted eleven trees:
cherry, maple, apple, and ash,
one for each grandchild.

In his pocket he keeps
a handkerchief
in case she cries

beside him in the pew.

When you journey
50 years together
you know what to offer
the one you love.

YOU SHOULD TRY IT SOMETIME

From patriarch
to preschooler
we take turns stretching
out on water—
bodies like boats,
arms thrown back,
feet pointed heavenward,
and float down Cousin Creek
like oak leaves.

You should try it sometime.

Go on a day when sun
kisses your shoulders,
and cast yourself
like a line
into the spray
until you find
surrender suspends you,
body carried by current,
all your resistance
released to the river.

INSTRUCTIONS ON WASHING DISHES

"Wash glasses first,"
she said with seriousness
that day as we
stood by the sink
in her kitchen,
"They are cleanest, dearie,
and won't muddy the water."

"Next, do silverware,"
more unsolicited advice
that has proven valuable.

"After that, wipe small plates
and bowls."

Her kitchen
was her throne room
and each meal
was part holy offering
and part holy decree.

When dining at her table
it was best
to clean your plate
and consume seconds, if offered.
(They were always offered.)

Blueberry cram,
oreo cake,
chicken à la king,
chicken Divan,
recipes I still read

in her scrawling cursive.

Women of my generation
work outside the home.
We tell each other
real work happens
on spreadsheets,
in board rooms,
in brightly lit laboratories.

What would Grandma
say to that?
"Nonsense!"
and if you tasted her lasagna
you might agree.

HOLY EXERCISES

I bend to pick up towel
child tossed on floor,
to collect single socks
scattered in corners,
to gather cards
dropped by tired toddler,
to wipe water
puddling on wood.

I bend to watch movies
that bore me,
to reread that story,
to toileting that interrupts
another meal,
to tantrums that interfere
with my timetable,
to cries for comfort
that wake me.

You knelt to scrub
sandy soles
of the ones
whose DNA you threaded;
at Gethsemane
you fell to the ground
under the weight
of that pure will.

Let my daily training
make me pliable
that I might bend
more and more
to Love.

GRANDMA, WE BROKE ANOTHER OF YOUR DISHES TONIGHT

I imagined you wincing
as my 9-year-old
tried to open the door
with one hand on the plate.

Pieces of white porcelain
scattered across the porch.

This was from your Mikasa dish set,
the one with a navy ring circling the edge.

I know, we were always breaking your things.

Lamps, vases, glasses,
bringing chaos
into your well-ordered life.

Pebbles blanketed your cottage lawn instead of grass.
We threw the stones into your lagoon
to hear the plopping sound.

"Those rocks aren't free," you would say,
"a nickel a rock!"
Today you would charge more.

Tonight's culprit, my redhead, felt bad.
I do not care about the plate,
but it is one more
      connection   to you

severed.

I would like to walk into your shore house
one more time
at cocktail hour
my skin salty with seawater,
hear the screen door slap behind me,

smell lemon bars baking in your kitchen,
sit on your patio
by the lagoon
over a small wooden bowl
of oyster crackers
and listen to one of your stories.

TEA PARTY

My husband poured
black tea
into porcelain cups
while he broke the news
about his diagnosis.

My son scooped spoonfuls
of sugar and stirred.
My daughter dropped
milk into her mixture
and watched clouds appear.

I sipped Earl Grey,
kept my eyes
on our youngest
fumbling the fine china,
imagined shards
scattering like bones
across the kitchen floor,
saw myself holding a broom
sweeping pieces
into piles,
burying them
in the trash.

Our lives are china tea cups
in the hands of a toddler.

DOLLHOUSE

My daughter fingers
a figure who walks
toward dolls lying on a bunk
and calls,
"Wake up everyone!"

She plays with a toy
I once made into
my mother, the same

my mother, my aunt
pretended was
their mother.

The same narrow rooms,
wood floors
my grandma
inhabited with her imagination.

They tell me my great-grandfather
first sanded this pine,
stroked white paint on trim.
It is for me now
as if my daughter
with her sweet, high voice
calls out across miles,
beyond

time,
past the grave,
beckoning generations of women
back to this spacious home

where we sit as girls
legs crossed on the floor,
laughing
in our shared shelter.

YOURS, THE DOOR WE WALK THROUGH

Yours, the hush of dawn,
window's frosty design,
daughter's dancing eyes
hovering overhead,
whining of wind.

Yours, the clattering kettle,
steam smoking from tea,
kiss of kiwi on lips,
crunch of toast on teeth,
walkway blocked by snow,
my rosy-cheeked boy
and the green shovel he grips,
fresh path he clears.

Yours, the slipperiness of ice,
sharpness of blades,
hill frosted white,
slip of sled down slope,
peal of laughter
that echoes through the plain.

Yours, the door we walk through
to warmth that wombs us,
to candle's panting breath,
to holy spits of stove,
exhale of sleeping child,
man holding my hand,
sweet spell of sleep.

LEARNING TO SWIM

—for Ewan

My boy dives underwater
and my body floats alongside him,
between surface and floor.

With eyes wide, he searches
pool's bottom for plastic pike
he can scoop in an orange net.

He sputters up, blinking,
water pouring down his cheeks,
grinning at me as if to say,

"I just learned to fly!"
holding out his catch
like he has snagged

in his one-dollar fishing net
a priceless secret of the universe.

DURING AN ARGUMENT

my daughter and I
strip down to our suits
and wade silently
into the swirling Lamoille.

River rushes
over rocks,
and I fumble to find
my footing
on the sandstone bed.

My firstborn slips
into the stream
and as she dips under
and rises up
I watch water
wash over her golden hair.

Before I know it
I too abandon body
to eddies
and coast on current
that carries me toward her.

My girl and I float downstream
bellies up,
toes pointing skyward,
pulled along on a
leash
of laughter.

FREE PARKING

Everything delights:
shoe squeaking on floor,
swish of blue gown
as it falls into bin,
sparkle in the sonographer's smile.

"Thank you," I say to the secretary,
as if she were sovereign,
and all these gifts the candy
showering down from her divine piñata.

As I drive out of the garage
the parking attendant looks down at me,
"It's free today," he says.

"Oh yes, I know," I reply.

LEARNING TO READ

—for Asher

The boy perches on a pew
built over a century ago
and shades a clipart cross brown
crayons yellow on sun
green on hill
while his Daddy preaches
about Mary weeping
by the empty tomb.

"Why do you look
for the living
among the dead?"
the angel asks her.
"He is not here."

The lad lays down his crayon,
studies letters on coloring page,
slides a finger under the H,
exhales a hush of air,
"Hah, ee," squeaks from his throat,
"H-e i-s ri-sen!" he reads,
his eyes, like Mary's, shining
with a glimpse of another world.

THE LAST DAY OF SUMMER

His hair grew
while he dug in dirt,
swung on swing,
paddled a kayak
on Lake Christopher,
boarded Atlantic waves,
rode wheelies.

I snip off clumps
and they tumble
soundlessly
to the porch floor.

There I go
scissoring off summer,
cutting through
campfire smoke,
first flips from diving board,
fear of dark water.

A lock of hair
flutters to the grass.

Breeze sweeps it past
white clover
and nestles it
in the side garden
next to the fuchsia Phlox.

TIME TRAVELER

I think I will travel back today
through the labyrinth of stages,
the web of regrets,
back before wounds
and worries
to when you rested
easy
in me,
your body
corded
to my body.

I wouldn't want to start over there
because child,
we're heading somewhere
you and me,
but I wouldn't mind a short trip,
a chance to hold you
without you minding
and to meet myself again too,
the stranger
who thought she knew
what there was to know
about love.

EVERY VERTEBRA ALIGNS

She spins around the bar,
casts her body and flips,
hangs upside down,
her long, blond hair sweeping the floor
like a flag of childhood.

She wants to be a gymnast
and her body seems to agree.
It already knows
how to balance,
flex,
fold,
lean and flip.

Each movement is music
as lovely as an orchestra
playing Brandenburg Concerto number three,
every tendon in her body
bending in harmony.

WHILE SCALING PATTEE HILL

in soft summer air
pebbles popped
from under Odyssey tires
as the old minivan whined
up the dirt road.

Under a sugar maple
near my friend's garden
a White-tailed deer
with her two fawns
froze.

I stopped the vehicle,
and imagined tiptoeing
toward the doe.

Perhaps we could start
a support group
this mother and I,
something simple:
Mammal Mothers Welcome.

We would meet
on the lawn
to talk about

the terror
that comes
with love.

DOMESTIC AFFAIRS

What would I give
for my son to pee
with the bathroom door closed?
I would pay millions
offer my body for research
spill my retirement
if only it might inspire
some slight behavior change.

What would I give
for this child
to wash his hands
without reminders
for a simple glance
in the mirror
at the peanut butter
that spreads from ear to ear?

What would
I give
for him
to smell his stench
and then sweetly
move to the shower?

If he were to shampoo
without needing threats
oh, the energy I would have!

I could pilot fighter jets
execute high-end Navy Seal missions
hike Everest backwards
on my knees.

WAITING ROOM

Sky-blue masks cover cheeks
and dimples. A man
thinned by lung cancer
sits in a wheelchair;
words grind from his mouth,
"Lost a lung my first
dance with cancer."

Meanwhile, my toddler
shakes her pigtails and smiles
an unmasked smile.

A nurse ushers us
to a room and my girl
twirls to her own tempo
while the doctor purses her lips
and feels lumps growing
under her father's armpits,
"These will not
go away," says the doctor.

My child opens drawers
in a medical dresser
while we discuss
white blood cells.

As the doctor schedules scans
and warns of internal nodes,
my girl unpacks my purse,
pausing to hear paper crinkle.

She carries wrappers to the trash,
sways to silent music
while we explore
Lymphocytes and spleen size.

Perhaps she knows more than we do.

WHAT CAN A MOTHER SAY TO THOSE EYES?

Driving down Mount Jay
through a snow squall
the Ford in front of us
lost traction
and skidded into a ditch.

While my husband helped victims
I faced
the Greek chorus
in the backseat.

Four sets of eyes
stared at me
asking,
"How could
     you
let this happen?"

Oh, my children,
how little you know
of the heartache
this world can hold
and how much
you overestimate
my power over it.

MAKE ME DRIFTWOOD

I have no muscle memory
for raising white flag
hand

       over

          hand

       fabric
cracking in wind
air ironing out crease
nylon flapping freely
from pole.

How do I learn
to let go?

Teach me, O Lord
to lie
long-bodied
on lake
fists
loosened
palms
flattened
limbs splayed
as waves

lift me
land me

like a piece

       of driftwood.

I TOLD MY THERAPIST ABOUT MY ANGER

practiced acceptance
of imperfect realities
in his air-conditioned office
and when I left the building
humidity hit me like a wall.

I walked into the house
to find the kids—and the kids' friends—
circling the kitchen like piranhas.
I tossed them ham sandwiches
and when they were fed
the request came:
Can we please
do a lemonade stand?

Before I knew it,
the neighborhood gang
had squeezed fresh lemons,
littered rinds on counter,
left the fridge open,
let the dog loose,
and spilled a sugar trail
on the laminate
that crunched
under my shoes
like sand.

The dog stole
my steaming sourdough.

Only a few hours
after breathing in and out
with my therapist
the house looked like
the scene of a horror movie
and I became a character in it.

I yelled at my children.
One of them cried.

Maybe next session
I will talk
about something else.

BENEATH SLANTED EAVES

cousins sprawl on bunks and trundles
listening to cicadas' hum,
smelling North Country air
scented with campfire,
water from an after-dinner swim
still wetting their hair,
the strong bones
of house
holding them.
Breath of others
lullabies them,
until their own inhales
lengthen
and stretch
into a shared web of dreams.

THE PARSONAGE ON PLAINS ROAD

Where locust litters leaves
after a storm,
hollyhocks lean westward,
hens squawk and peck,
and kids hawk lemonade.

Where Barred Owl
hoots a haunting call,
chickadees snack on sunflowers,
robins nurture nests
atop rafters,
and the children
running in and out
seldom remember to shut the door.

Where red paint flakes off the shed,
the young pop on Pogo sticks,
and the neighbor boy
waits on the rope swing
hoping for another push.

Where the bachelors next door
wander over and lean against the fence,
the doodle perches on the picnic table,
and our oaks continue their climb
up from earth.

CIRQUE KIKASSE

The night the circus came to town

clouds clumped
                    like cotton candy
air glided over shoulders
            like a silk gown

                    brassy sounds of sousaphone
            baptized crowd.

The doctor made his rounds
            among the people,
"How are you feeling, my friend?"

                    while children sucked in breath
            at jumping and juggling tricks
and at evening's end
        when   popcorn   dotted   dewy   grass

we all looked for the gaggle of girls

who had   slipped   off
perhaps they were

our   younger   selves.

REMEMBER

—for Chloe, Asher, Ewan, and Willa

The Lord watches over you;
he umbrellas you in rain,
lullabies you during nightmare,
belays you through rocky climb.

The Lord watches over you;
he is blaze painted on birch,
cairn piled above tree line
that compasses you onward.

The Lord watches over you;
He hummingbirds around you,
flashlights you through dark,
nets you in an invisible web.

The Lord watches over you;
he is railing on stairs,
cane in trembling hand,
salt sprinkled on icy walk.

The Lord watches over you;
he is motion sensor monitoring
danger at your doorway,
bolt sliding securely into steel frame.

Sons and daughters, whenever
you glimpse Green Mountains,
remember the One who chiseled
the marble, who acorned each oak.

I lift my eyes up to the mountains —

where does my help come from?

My help comes from the Lord,

the maker of heaven and earth,

he will not let your foot slip—

he who watches over you will not slumber;

indeed, he who watches over Israel

will neither slumber nor sleep.
—Psalm 121:1-4

ACKNOWLEDGMENTS

A TEAM OF PEOPLE COLLABORATED over the years to birth this book. To Wipf and Stock and my editor Matthew Wimer, thanks for giving *Child, I Will Always Carry You* a publishing home. My gratitude goes out to my early readers, Devon Parish, Jess Courtemanche, and Lauren Deitsch. Deborah Dickerson, fellow poet, you have been a first reader of many of these poems through the years. Without the Joy-Filled Scribblers this book would not exist. Michelle Wiegers, Gayle Heaslip, Jeremy Stefano, and Maria Roemhildt, your fellowship in writing and faith delight me. A huge debt of thanks to Abigail Carroll for writing exquisite poetry. Your "Make Me" poems and reflections on the psalms inspired poems in this collection. Thanks for generously pouring yourself into editing and finding potential in this manuscript. Kathleen Smith, thanks for always being in my corner and cheering me on as writer and mother.

Mom and Dad, you built a family where artists could flourish. The love you lavish continues to teach me how to love. Mom, thank you for carrying me all these years and for your joy in these poems. Dad, I remember when I was a child you often would say, "Meg, look at the sunset". Thank you for teaching me about beauty. I appreciate your investment in this manuscript.

Chloe, Asher, Ewan, and Willa, you are precious to me. Watching you grow and learn brings me deep joy. I am thankful for the privilege of carrying you.

Tyler, writing brought us together and I love all the ways we get to create together. Your belief in me as a poet empowered me to get started and has helped me to stay the course. You have been tech support, childcare provider, editor, copyeditor, etc. You deserve a stork pin for helping deliver this baby. I'm grateful we get to go through life as a team.

Acknowledgments

Thanks to the One who made me a mom, a writer, and most importantly, a child of God. Your love sustains me. All the wonder, beauty, and goodness in this world come from You.